W9-CKH-295

The Boxcar Children Cookbook

by Diane Blain

Illustrated by
L. Kate Deal and Eileen Mueller Neill

Albert Whitman & Company, Morton Grove, Illinois

To Jody, who loves to eat,
and Jessica, who is still learning to cook.

Special thanks to
Shirley Neitzel and Don Blain for all their encouraging support and help in the writing of this book, and to my Kettle Lake Elementary School students for being such enthusiastic beginning cooks.

Thanks to the Michigan State University
Cooperative Extension Service for information on outdoor cooking, measuring, cooking terms, and safety in the kitchen.

Published in 1991 by Albert Whitman & Company, Morton Grove, Illinois 60053-2723.
Published simultaneously in Canada by General Publishing, Limited, Toronto.
 Printed in the U.S.A.
10 9 8 7 6 5 4 3

Edited by Betty Modaressi.
Designed by Eileen Mueller Neill.

Library of Congress Cataloging-in-Publication Data

Blain, Diane.
The Boxcar Children Cookbook / by Diane Blain.
p. cm.
Includes index.
Summary: A collection of recipes based on the meals eaten by the Boxcar Children in the series of books describing their mysterious adventures.
ISBN 0-8075-0859-4 lib. bdg. 0-8075-0856-X pbk.
1. Cookery—Juvenile literature. [1. Cookery. 2. Literary cookbooks.] I. Title.
TX652.5.B53 1991 91-15080
641.5'123—dc20 CIP
AC

Table of Contents

Cooking with the Boxcar Children

The Boxcar Children love to cook! At first, when Henry, Jessie, Violet, and Benny lived in the boxcar, they had to cook because there was no one else to cook for them. Now that they are living with Grandfather Alden, they cook because they like to.

You will find many of their favorite recipes in this cookbook. Just follow a few simple kitchen rules, and you can have as much fun cooking as the Boxcar Children do.

Before you start, check with an adult in your family to see if it's a good time for you to cook. Ask him or her to read the recipe with you to see that you have everything you need. You may need grown-up help to make some foods, especially if you are going to use a sharp knife or an appliance. Be sure you have enough time to prepare the food and cook it. Set out all the equipment and ingredients you'll be using so that you won't forget anything. Check to see that everything you'll use is very clean—including your hands. And remember—clean up the kitchen when you finish.

Your family and friends will be very impressed to see food you've cooked yourself. And you'll all have a wonderful time eating it!

Safety First!

When you work in the kitchen, you have to be very careful not to cut or burn yourself. Follow these safety rules so that you'll stay safe and have fun cooking Boxcar recipes.

1. Ask for help from an adult when you use a can opener, microwave oven, electric mixer, blender, or sharp knife.
2. Be sure to pick up a sharp knife by the handle, not the blade. Before you cut anything, see that the blade is facing down. Wash sharp knives separately—not with other dishes.
3. When you use a vegetable peeler, peel away from yourself.
4. Ask an adult to drain water from hot foods like spaghetti and the fat from meat. Even the steam from these foods can cause severe burns.
5. Use thick, dry potholders or oven mitts.
6. If you have long hair, tie it back. Roll up long sleeves so that they won't get caught on a pan handle or drag across a burner.
7. Turn the handles of pans toward the center of the stove so that you don't bump them and tip the pans over.
8. If you use a blender or mixer, be sure your hands are dry before plugging it in. Turn it off before you scrape the sides of the container or bowl. Unplug the mixer before you put the beaters in or take them out. Never put anything electrical in water.
9. If a small fire flares up in a pan, put the lid on the pan. This will smother the flames. Sprinkling baking soda on a fire will also smother it. Never pour water on a grease fire since water will only make the fire spread.
10. Never leave the kitchen when a burner is turned on "high."

When You Use the Stove or Oven

To cook many of the Boxcar Children Recipes, you will need to use a stovetop, an oven, or a microwave oven. Ask an adult to help you when you use any of these appliances.

Range or Stovetop

Put small pans on small burners and large pans on large burners. Turn pan handles toward the center of the stove (but not over other burners) so that you don't bump them and tip the pans over. Be sure to turn off burners when you finish using them.

Oven

Before you turn the oven on, be sure the rack you are going to use is placed in the center. Don't let pans in the oven touch each other. If a recipe tells you to bake the food covered, cover the baking dish with aluminum foil or a tight-fitting lid. Always use thick, dry oven mitts or potholders to take food out of the oven.

Microwave Oven

Read the instruction book that came with your microwave oven. Follow all directions in the book. Do not use anything that is metal or trimmed with metal in the microwave oven. Hot food can make the dishes very hot, so use potholders or oven mitts to remove dishes from the microwave oven. If the food you are cooking needs to be covered, follow the directions in the recipe. Let food sit for 2 or 3 minutes after you remove it from the microwave oven. It will finish cooking as it sits.

Measure Up!

Not all recipe ingredients are measured the same way. Here are some tips to help you measure right.

Flour and white sugar: Dip a dry measuring cup into the container and level it off with the straight edge of a knife or spatula.

Brown sugar: Pack the brown sugar into a dry measuring cup with a spoon and then level it off with the straight edge of a knife or spatula.

Baking powder, baking soda, salt, and spices: Dip the measuring spoon into the ingredient and level it off.

Shredded cheese, shredded coconut, bread crumbs, chocolate chips, raisins, and nuts: Pack lightly into a dry measuring cup until level.

Margarine: Margarine stick wrappers have marks to show tablespoons and parts of cups.

Vegetable oil, water, milk, and other liquids: Set liquid measuring cup on the counter. Pour in the liquid, and then bend down to check the amount at eye level.

Vanilla and other liquid flavorings: Carefully pour the liquid into a measuring spoon.

Beverages

After a day of exciting adventures, the Boxcar Children are hungry and thirsty. They know how to make beverages that just hit the spot. Try some of these drinks from the Boxcar Children mysteries and have some new taste treats!

Snowbound Hot Chocolate Mix

(6 servings)

After walking in the cold, deep snow, the Alden children finally reached the cabin in *Snowbound Mystery.* Then they were snowed in! Jessie knew that hot chocolate would warm them all up.

What to Use

2 cups non-fat dry milk
1/4 cup unsweetened cocoa
1/4 cup sugar

measuring cups
mixing bowl
mixing spoon
quart jar with lid

What to Do

1. Mix all dry ingredients together.
2. Store in a covered jar and use as needed.

What to Use to Make Hot Chocolate

boiling water
1/3 cup hot chocolate mix
1 marshmallow (if wanted)

teakettle
measuring cup
cup or mug
spoon
wire whisk

What to Do

1. For each serving, put 1/3 cup mix into a cup or mug.
2. Fill the cup or mug with boiling water. Stir.
3. Add 1 marshmallow (if wanted).

To make all 6 servings, add 6 cups of boiling water to all of the mix in a large saucepan. Stir with a wire whisk.

Pomfret Landing Milkshake

(1 serving)

In *Houseboat Mystery*, the Alden children went into the candy store in Pomfret Landing and watched candy being made. Afterward, they decided to have strawberry milkshakes.

What to Use

3/4 cup milk
1 scoop vanilla ice cream
2 Tablespoons strawberry jam*
1 Tablespoon instant vanilla pudding mix

blender
measuring cup
measuring spoons
ice cream scoop
tall glass

What to Do

1. Pour milk into the blender container.
2. Add ice cream, jam, and pudding mix.
3. Cover tightly and blend until mixed well.
4. Pour your milkshake into a tall glass and enjoy.

*If you would like to make a chocolate- or caramel-flavored milkshake, use two tablespoons of chocolate or caramel ice cream topping in place of the jam.

Maggie's Lemonade

(8 servings)

The family all sat around the long table to eat lunch. Maggie had sent up a large basket of sandwiches and salad and pink lemonade with ice in it. —Mike's Mystery

What to Use

1 cup sugar
1 cup lemon juice
(or 4 large or 6 small lemons)
2 quarts water
1/4 cup red cherry juice
ice cubes

fruit juicer
measuring cup
large pitcher
mixing spoon
tall glasses

What to Do

1. If you are using fresh lemons, squeeze the juice from enough lemons to make 1 cup of juice.
2. Mix sugar, lemon juice, and water in a large pitcher.
3. Add cherry juice if you want to make your lemonade pink.
4. Pour the lemonade over ice cubes in tall glasses.

Caboose Orange Special

(1 serving)

On the way to Pinedale from the glass factory in *Caboose Mystery*, Jessie had a new idea for punch. She had some cola and orange juice left from the train trip and decided to put them together to make a new party drink.

What to Use

3 ice cubes
1/2 cup orange juice
(or 2 oranges)
1/2 cup cola

fruit juicer
measuring cup
tall glass

What to Do

1. If you are using fresh oranges, squeeze the juice from 2 of them.
2. Pour orange juice over the ice cubes in the glass.
3. Pour cola into the glass. Stir.

You can make a good party punch by substituting ginger ale or lemon-lime soda for the cola in this recipe.

Jessie's Eggnog

(1 serving)

When Grandfather visited the Boxcar Children in *Surprise Island*, Jessie fixed him a delicious drink of milk, eggs, and sugar.

What to Use

1 egg
2 Tablespoons sugar
1 cup cold milk
1/4 teaspoon vanilla
1 dash nutmeg

measuring cup
measuring spoons
small saucepan with lid
wire whisk
glass or plastic bowl
plastic wrap

What to Do

1. Put egg, sugar, and milk in the saucepan. Mix with wire whisk.
2. Cook over medium heat, stirring constantly until the egg mixture starts to coat the whisk or begins to steam. Do NOT let the mixture boil or it may curdle. Stir in vanilla.
3. Pour the mixture into a glass or plastic bowl and cover with plastic wrap. Cool in the refrigerator. Before serving, stir with a wire whisk. Sprinkle on nutmeg.

How to Microwave

1. Use a plastic or glass bowl. Follow step #1.
2. Remove the whisk. Cook the mixture in the microwave oven on high for 1 1/2 minutes. Stir. Cook 1 1/2 minutes longer. Stir in vanilla.
3. Cool in the refrigerator. Before serving, stir and sprinkle on nutmeg.

Breads

Nothing tops the smell of homemade bread baking in the oven, and bread tastes great with any meal. The Boxcar Children think that sometimes just bread and butter with a glass of milk make a good meal.

Boxcar Brown Bread

(2 loaves)

When Henry came, he had some heavy bundles. He had four bottles of milk in a bag, a loaf of brown bread, and also some fine yellow cheese. —The Boxcar Children

What to Use

3 cups raisin bran cereal
1 stick softened margarine
1 cup hot water
1 1/2 cups brown sugar
2 eggs
3 cups flour
2 1/2 teaspoons baking soda
2 cups milk
2 teaspoons lemon juice
1 1/2 teaspoons cinnamon
2 more cups raisin bran cereal

2 bread pans (8 1/2" x 4 1/2")
no-stick cooking spray
large mixing bowl
measuring cups
measuring spoons
wire whisk or electric mixer
rubber scraper
toothpick
wire cooling rack

What to Do

1. Preheat the oven to 350 degrees.
2. Spray the bread pans with no-stick cooking spray. Set aside.
3. Pour hot water over the first 3 cups of cereal and margarine in a mixing bowl.
4. Add brown sugar, eggs, flour, baking soda, milk, lemon juice, and cinnamon.
5. Mix with a wire whisk or electric mixer until smooth.
6. Mix in the last 2 cups of bran cereal.
7. Pour the batter, evenly divided, into the bread pans.
8. Put the pans into the oven. Bake for 50 minutes. Poke a toothpick into the center of the bread and then pull it out. If the toothpick comes out clean, the bread is done. If not, bake the bread for 5 to 10 minutes more and test again. Use oven mitts to remove the bread from the oven.
9. Let the bread cool in the pans for 10 minutes. Then turn the pans upside down. The bread should fall out of the pans. Let the bread cool on a wire rack.
10. When the bread is cool, put each loaf into a plastic bag. It will be easier to cut the day after it is baked — if you can wait that long to eat it!

This recipe can also be made into 2 1/2 dozen muffins. Bake them in paper-lined cups for 20 minutes at 350 degrees. Be sure to test them with a toothpick to see if they are done.

Campout Cornbread

(9 servings)

In *The Yellow House Mystery*, camping out was really an adventure for the Aldens. The fresh air made everyone hungry. Mr. Hill showed them how to make ham, eggs, and cornbread.

What to Use

1 1/4 cups flour
3/4 cup cornmeal
1/4 cup sugar
2 teaspoons baking powder
1/2 teaspoon salt
1 cup milk
1/4 cup vegetable oil
1 egg

mixing bowl
mixing spoon
measuring cups
measuring spoons
8" x 8" baking pan
no-stick cooking spray
toothpick

What to Do

1. Preheat the oven to 400 degrees.
2. Spray the baking pan with no-stick cooking spray.
3. Mix all ingredients together in a mixing bowl.
4. Pour the mixture into the baking pan.
5. Bake 18-20 minutes or until a toothpick comes out clean when poked into the center. Remove from the oven.
6. Cut into squares and serve warm with margarine.

Lovan's Corn Muffins

(12 muffins)

You can also make corn muffins like the ones Lovan made in *Mountain Top Mystery*. Use the recipe for Campout Cornbread, but pour the batter into 12 muffin papers in a muffin pan. Bake at 400 degrees for 15 minutes. Test with a toothpick.

Sea Biscuits

(28-30 sea biscuits)

When Lars and the children were packing food for their trip in *Blue Bay Mystery,* Lars packed sea biscuits. Mike didn't understand what sea biscuits were, but he soon found out.

What to Use

1 cup flour
1/2 teaspoon salt
1 teaspoon baking powder
2 Tablespoons softened margarine
1/4 cup warm water

mixing bowl
measuring cups
measuring spoons
fork
cookie sheet

What to Do

1. Preheat the oven to 425 degrees.
2. Put all ingredients in the mixing bowl and mix with a fork until the mixture has lumps the size of peas.
3. Work the dough with your hands until it is smooth.
4. Divide the dough into 28-30 small pieces about the size of marbles.
5. Roll each piece of dough into a ball and then flatten it with your fingers into a very thin circle.
6. Place the circles on an ungreased cookie sheet.
7. Bake in the oven 8-10 minutes or until the biscuits are dry and light brown around the edges.
8. Cool and store in an airtight container.

Sea biscuits taste especially good served with strawberry preserves or your favorite jelly.

Secret Code Buns

(30 small buns)

1M 1/4B 1/4S 1S 1Y
1/4W 1E ? 3F R
400: 15

Benny found this code in the cabin in *Snowbound Mystery.* It was the secret recipe that Tom's father used to make his special buns. You can make buns like those, but you won't have to use as many ingredients. If you want to see what the code stands for, look on page 95 in *Snowbound Mystery.*

What to Use

1 Tablespoon flour
2 loaves frozen sweet roll dough
1/2 cup raisins

measuring cups
measuring spoons
plastic wrap
knife
9" x 13" cake pan
large plastic bag
cookie sheet

Secret Ingredients

1/2 cup margarine
1/2 cup brown sugar
1/2 cup chopped nuts (if wanted)

Cinnamon-Sugar Mixture
2 teaspoons cinnamon
2 Tablespoons sugar

Tom's father wrote his bun recipe in code because he wanted to keep it a secret. What code could you use to keep your bun recipe a secret?

What to Do

1. Thaw the sweet roll dough.
2. Sprinkle flour on the counter and put the dough and raisins on top of it. Work as many raisins as you can into the dough. Work the dough with your hands for 2 or 3 minutes.
3. Cover the dough with plastic wrap and let it rest during the next step—about 20 minutes. The dough will rise.
4. Use secret ingredients to prepare the baking pan. Melt margarine in the cake pan over very low heat. Remove from heat. Add brown sugar and stir until well mixed. Sprinkle chopped nuts over the mixture. Set the pan aside until it is needed.
5. Return to the dough that has been rising. Remove plastic wrap and cut the dough into 30 small balls.
6. Put cinnamon and white sugar into the large plastic bag. Shake the balls (3 at a time) in the bag and put them into the prepared pan.
7. Let the buns rise in a warm place until they have doubled in size. This will take about 1 hour.
8. Preheat the oven to 400 degrees. Bake the buns 15 minutes.
9. Use oven mitts to remove the pan from the oven. Let the buns cool in the pan for 10 minutes.
10. Ask an adult to do this step. Place a cookie sheet over the buns. Using oven mitts, carefully flip the pan so that the cake pan is upside down and the buns are on the cookie sheet, covered with the melted topping. Serve the buns warm.

Baker's Bread in a Bag

(1 loaf)

Henry cut one of the loaves of bread into four pieces with his knife, and the children began to eat. —The Boxcar Children

What to Use

1 package (1/4 ounce) yeast
1 1/2 cups flour
1 Tablespoon sugar
1 teaspoon salt
2 Tablespoons margarine
1 cup very warm water
1 1/2 more cups flour
(extra flour if needed)

self-sealing zip-type plastic bag (1 gallon size)
measuring cups
measuring spoons
bread pan
no-stick cooking spray

What to Do

1. Put yeast, 1 1/2 cups flour, sugar, and salt into the bag.
2. Add margarine and warm water. Press most of the air out of the bag and seal. Press and squeeze the bag with your hands until the dough becomes mixed.
3. Open bag and add last 1 1/2 cups of flour. Seal the bag again and keep pressing and squeezing until the flour is worked into the dough. Add 1/4 to 1/2 cup more flour if your dough is very sticky.
4. Unzip the bag and let the dough rest for 20 minutes. This will let the dough rise.
5. Spray the pan with no-stick cooking spray. Squeeze the dough down. Then take the dough out of the bag and place it in the pan. Let the dough rest in the pan in a warm, but not hot, place to rise. The dough should double its size before baking. This will take about 1 hour.
6. Preheat the oven to 375 degrees. Bake the bread for 25-30 minutes. Remove the bread from the pan to cool.

Breakfast

Henry, Jessie, Violet, and Benny know that breakfast is a very important meal. A good breakfast gives them the energy they need to work hard and think fast. Try some of these great Boxcar breakfasts before you go to school or head out to explore. They're quick and easy to make, and they'll get your day started off right.

Early-Riser Hot Cereals

(1 serving each)

The Boxcar Children always eat big breakfasts, even when they are away from home. On the canoe trip in *The Yellow House Mystery*, Mr. Hill made them a breakfast of bacon, quick bread, and cereal.

Try some of these hot cereals. You can cook your cereal on the stove or in the microwave oven and have a satisfying, fast breakfast.

What to Use

for Stovetop Cooking

small saucepan with lid
measuring cups
measuring spoons
mixing spoon
cereal bowl

for Microwave Oven Cooking

large (2-cup) cereal bowl*
measuring cups
measuring spoons
mixing spoon

Oatmeal: 3/4 cup water + 1/3 cup dry quick oatmeal
Hasty Pudding: 2/3 cup water + 3 Tablespoons dry cornmeal
Grits: 3/4 cup water + 3 Tablespoons dry grits
Cream of Wheat: 3/4 cup water + 2 Tablespoons dry cream of wheat
Cream of Rice: 3/4 cup water + 3 Tablespoons dry cream of rice

*When cooking cereal in the microwave oven, be sure to use a large bowl because cereals boil up and may overflow a smaller bowl.

What to Do for Stovetop Cooking

1. Measure water and dry cereal into small saucepan. Stir.
2. Bring to a boil over medium heat.
3. Turn off heat. Stir again. Cover the pan.
4. Wait for 3 minutes, and then pour the cereal into a bowl and add your favorite topping.
5. For easy cleanup after pouring out the cereal, put 1/2 cup water into the pan and cover. This will keep the cereal from drying out and sticking to the pan.

What to Do for Microwave Cooking

1. Mix cereal and hot water in a large cereal bowl.
2. Microwave uncovered on high for 1 1/2 to 2 minutes, stirring halfway through the cooking time.
3. Let the cereal stand for two minutes, and then add your favorite topping.

Tasty Toppings for Cereal

Margarine and Brown Sugar: Put 1 teaspoon margarine on your hot cereal. Top with 1 Tablespoon brown sugar. Stir.

Ice Cream Cool-Off: Scoop a Tablespoonful of your favorite ice cream over your hot cereal. It tastes delicious and cools off your cereal quickly for those hurry-up breakfasts.

Apple-Cinnamon: Add 1 Tablespoon cool applesauce and a sprinkle of cinnamon to your hot cereal.

Mystery Ranch French Toast

(6 servings)

The girls put pieces of dry bread in the eggs and milk, and Jessie began to brown them in the pan. —Mystery Ranch

What to Use

2 eggs
1/2 cup milk
1/2 teaspoon vanilla
6 slices stale bread
1 Tablespoon margarine
margarine and syrup

griddle or electric frying pan
measuring cup
measuring spoons
mixing bowl
fork
pancake turner

What to Do

1. Preheat the griddle over medium heat, or set the electric frying pan at 375 degrees.
2. Put eggs, milk, and vanilla in the mixing bowl and beat with a fork until well mixed.
3. Grease the griddle or pan with a thin layer of margarine.
4. Dip both sides of bread, one slice at a time, in the egg mixture and cook on the hot griddle or frying pan.
5. Cook until golden brown. This will take about 4 minutes on each side.
6. Turn the toast over with the pancake turner to cook the other side. Serve with margarine and syrup.

Aunt Jane's Milk Toast

You can make milk toast like Jessie made for Aunt Jane. Put a piece of toast in a shallow bowl and slowly pour 1/3 cup of warm milk over it. Sprinkle it with salt and pepper.

Hen's Nest Scrambled Eggs

(1 or 2 servings)

The eggs made a delicious supper. Jessie put them in a bowl with a little salt, and Violet took a spoon and stirred them as hard as she could.

"Put in some milk, Violet," said Jessie, "and stir them some more."

— The Boxcar Children

What to Use

2 eggs
2 Tablespoons milk
1 teaspoon margarine
salt
pepper

small mixing bowl
measuring spoons
fork
small frying pan
large stirring spoon

What to Do

1. Put eggs and milk in the small mixing bowl and mix with a fork until well blended.
2. Heat margarine in the frying pan over medium heat until it begins to bubble but not turn brown.
3. Pour in the egg mixture and turn heat down to low. Cook the eggs slowly, stirring them constantly.
4. Be sure the eggs cook thoroughly. You can tell that the eggs are cooked when they look completely dry.
5. Sprinkle lightly with salt and pepper before serving.

Mrs. Cole's Hard-Boiled Eggs

(1 egg for each serving)

In *The Woodshed Mystery*, Benny was surprised when Mrs. Cole told him that she always had cold eggs for her family because they liked cold hard-boiled eggs for breakfast.

What to Use

eggs (1 for each serving)
water

saucepan with lid

What to Do

1. Put as many eggs as you want to cook in a saucepan. Pour enough cold water in the pan to go just over the tops of the eggs. Put the lid on the pan.
2. Turn the burner on high and cook just until the water boils. Turn off the heat, but keep the lid on the pan. Wait 20 minutes.
3. Carefully set the pan in the sink and run cold water over the eggs to cool them quickly. This keeps the yolks from turning dark around the edges and makes the eggs easier to shell.
4. To shell the eggs easily, tap each one on the countertop or sink to crack the shell all over. Roll the egg gently between your hands to loosen the shell. Run cold water over it as you peel the egg.

Telegram Ham

(1/2 to 1 slice for each person)

"Come on, let's eat!" said Benny. "Can't you smell the ham and eggs, Grandfather? Don't you feel hungry now?" —Mystery Ranch

What to Use

1/2 to 1 slice of ham
for each person

frying pan
no-stick cooking spray
pancake turner

What to Do

1. Spray the inside of the frying pan with no-stick cooking spray.
2. Put ham slices in the frying pan.
3. Over medium heat, brown both sides of the ham slices.

Explorer's Bacon

What to Use

bacon
(2 slices for each serving)

microwave oven
glass plate
paper towels

What to Do

1. Put 2 layers of paper towels on the plate.
2. Put bacon in rows on the paper towels.
3. Cover bacon slices with another paper towel.
4. Microwave on high for 1 minute for each slice.

Serve your ham or bacon with Mystery Ranch French Toast, Hen's Nest Scrambled Eggs, or Canoe-Trip Pancakes.

Canoe-Trip Pancakes

(9 pancakes)

"Breakfast!" called Cookie, ringing the bell. Soon the men were eating great plates of quick bread. But Cookie had made beautiful brown pancakes for the visitors. They ate them with butter and brown sugar. —The Yellow House Mystery

What to Use

1 cup flour
1 Tablespoon sugar
2 Tablespoons margarine, melted
1 Tablespoon baking powder
3/4 cup milk
1 egg

mixing bowl
measuring cups
measuring spoons
wire whisk
griddle
pastry brush
pancake turner

What to Do

1. Put all ingredients into the bowl and mix with the whisk until smooth. If you want thinner pancakes, add 2 Tablespoons more milk.
2. Heat the griddle over medium heat until drops of water, when sprinkled on it, dance on the surface.
3. Use margarine and the pastry brush to grease griddle.
4. For each pancake, pour about 1/4 cup pancake batter on the griddle. Don't let the sides of the pancakes touch each other.
5. When the pancakes have lots of bubbles on the top and they have started to brown underneath, flip them over with the pancake turner and brown the other sides.

Pancakes are good with margarine and syrup, brown sugar, or your favorite jam or jelly.

Sandwiches

There's nothing better than a sandwich for a quick lunch or supper while you're busy exploring. Here are recipes for some of the sandwiches in the Boxcar Children books. The sandwiches are basic and simple, and you can even make your own peanut butter.

Benny's #1 Favorite Sandwich (Peanut Butter)

(about 2 cups of peanut butter)

Very soon they were all sitting at a big table for lunch. "Oh, peanut butter!" cried Benny. "I thought I'd never see you again!"
—Blue Bay Mystery

What to Use

1 pound roasted peanuts
1/2 teaspoon salt
(if wanted)
1 or 2 Tablespoons corn oil
or peanut oil

blender
measuring spoons
rubber scraper
pint jar with lid

What to Do

1. Put peanuts, salt (if wanted), and 1 Tablespoon oil in the blender container.
2. Place the cover on the blender and start at low speed.
3. When the peanuts are chopped, switch to a higher speed. Blend 10 seconds. Stop the blender. Scrape down sides of the container with a rubber scraper. Continue doing this step until the peanut butter is as smooth as you like.
4. Add more oil if you want creamier peanut butter. If your blender is too small to grind up all the peanuts at once, make smaller batches. Each batch should take between 5 and 10 minutes.
5. Use a rubber scraper to take your peanut butter out of the blender. Store the peanut butter in a covered pint jar in the refrigerator.

To make Benny's favorite sandwich, spread one slice of bread with peanut butter. Spread on a layer of jam or jelly. Then put another slice of bread on top. Enjoy!

Egg Salad Sandwiches

(4 sandwiches)

After Violet and Benny explored the house and the barn in *The Woodshed Mystery*, they were hungry and wanted sandwiches. They got good sandwiches from Sim and his wife.

What to Use

3 hard-boiled eggs
1/3 cup chopped celery
1 teaspoon chopped onion
3 Tablespoons mayonnaise
1/4 teaspoon salt
(if wanted)
8 slices bread

cutting board
sharp knife
measuring cup
small mixing bowl
measuring spoons
mixing spoon
table knife

What to Do

1. Peel the eggs. Chop the eggs with a sharp knife and put them into the mixing bowl.
2. Chop celery and onion. Add to the eggs.
3. Add mayonnaise and salt (if wanted). Mix well.
4. Divide the egg mixture among 4 slices of bread. Spread with a table knife. Cover with the remaining slices of bread. Cut each sandwich into halves and serve. Cover any leftover sandwiches and refrigerate them.

Woodshed Chicken Salad Sandwiches

(4 sandwiches)

To make chicken salad sandwiches, use 2 cups of chopped, cooked chicken instead of the eggs. Then follow the directions for making egg salad sandwiches.

Violet's Tuna Sandwiches

(3 or 4 sandwiches)

Before going out to explore another mystery, the Alden children, at the urging of Benny, decided to eat lunch first.

"A good idea," said Violet. "I'd like a tuna fish sandwich. I hope we brought a can opener." —Snowbound Mystery

What to Use

1 can (7 ounces) tuna, drained
2 Tablespoons pickle relish
1/3 cup mayonnaise
bread
lettuce leaves

can opener
measuring cup
measuring spoons
fork
small mixing bowl

What to Do

1. Put tuna, pickle relish, and mayonnaise in the mixing bowl and stir with a fork until well mixed.
2. Spread a spoonful of the tuna mixture on a slice of bread. Top with a lettuce leaf and another slice of bread. Cut in halves or quarters.

Jim's Place Hamburgers

(4 hamburgers)

"Oh, hamburger!" yelled Benny. "I want hamburger!" "So do I," laughed Jessie. —The Yellow House Mystery

What to Use

1 pound ground beef
1 small onion, chopped
1/4 teaspoon pepper
4 hamburger buns

cutting board
sharp knife
mixing bowl
mixing spoon
measuring spoons
frying pan
pancake turner

What to Do

1. Chop the onion and put it into the mixing bowl.
2. Add ground beef and pepper. Mix well.
3. Shape the mixture into 4 hamburger patties.
4. Put hamburger patties into the frying pan and cook over medium heat. When hamburgers are browned on one side, turn them over with the pancake turner. Continue cooking until both sides are done. This should take 8 to 10 minutes for each side.
5. Serve hamburger patties on buns. Add condiments and other ingredients you like on hamburgers.

Condiments and other ingredients for hamburgers

cheese	ketchup	mustard	sliced olives
pickles	mayonnaise	relish	bacon bits
lettuce	tomatoes	mushrooms	sliced onion

Maggie's Hot Dogs

(4 servings)

"What is it?" asked Benny.

"Hot dogs," said Maggie. "Your Aunt Jane says all young people like hot dogs."

"We do!" cried Benny. "And we don't get them very often. Hurrah for Aunt Jane!" —Mike's Mystery

What to Use

4 hot dogs
1/2 cup water
4 hot dog buns

medium saucepan with lid
measuring cup
tongs

What to Do

1. Put hot dogs and water in the pan. Cover.
2. Turn the burner on high and bring the water to a boil.
3. Turn heat to low and simmer the hot dogs for 5 minutes.
4. Remove hot dogs with the tongs and put them on the buns. Add any condiments you like.

Condiments for hot dogs

ketchup mustard relish chopped onions

How to Microwave

Pierce each hot dog 3 times with a fork. Put the hot dogs in buns and wrap each one with a paper towel. Put the hot dogs on a paper plate and cook on high 1 minute for each hot dog.

Main Dishes, Soups, and Stews

The Aldens know that it is important for the family to get together at mealtimes. They talk about their day and plan future adventures. Make one of the Boxcar soups for lunch, or make a stew or main dish for supper. Everyone in your family will enjoy a delicious meal and be impressed because you made it all yourself.

Jessie's Clam Chowder

(4-6 servings)

"Yum, yum! Jessie can make good chowder!" said Benny.
—Surprise Island

What to Use

1 slice bacon, diced
1 small onion, chopped
1 cup peeled cubed potatoes
2 cups water
1 can (6 1/2 ounces) minced clams
2 cups milk
3 Tablespoons margarine, melted
2 Tablespoons flour
1/2 teaspoon salt
1/4 teaspoon pepper

large saucepan with lid
cutting board
knife
measuring cups
measuring spoons
can opener
stirring spoon

What to Do

1. Cook bacon in the large saucepan over low heat until crisp.
2. Add onion and cook until it is soft.
3. Carefully add potatoes and water. Turn the heat up to high and bring to a boil. Turn the heat down to medium and cook until the potatoes are done. This should take about 20 minutes.
4. Add clams and cook 2 minutes.
5. Add milk and cook 5 minutes.
6. Mix melted margarine, flour, salt, and pepper together. Add to the chowder. Cook, stirring constantly until the chowder is thick and hot. Serve immediately.

New Neighbor Casserole

(6 servings)

Everyone began to work. Benny opened cans of tomato soup. Henry peeled onions and cut them up. Violet got out some hamburger and began to break it up to cook in a pan. Jessie cooked macaroni and got out the cheese. —Tree House Mystery

What to Use

1 pound ground beef
1 medium onion, chopped
1/4 teaspoon pepper
2 Tablespoons parsley, chopped
1 clove garlic, crushed
2 cans tomato soup (10 1/2 ounces each)
1 soup can of water
1 1/2 cups elbow macaroni
8 ounces shredded cheddar cheese

large saucepan with lid
knife
pancake turner
cutting board
can opener
mixing spoon
measuring cups
measuring spoons
2-quart casserole dish
no-stick cooking spray

What to Do

1. Cook ground beef and onion in the large pan, breaking the beef apart with a pancake turner, until the beef loses its red color. Drain off fat.
2. Add pepper, parsley, garlic, soup, water, and uncooked macaroni. Stir to mix well.
3. Over medium heat, bring the mixture to a boil. Stir. Cover and turn heat down to low. Simmer for 20 minutes.
4. Spray casserole dish with no-stick cooking spray.
5. Pour ground beef and macaroni mixture into the casserole.
6. Sprinkle cheese on top. Keep your covered casserole in the oven on warm (200 degrees) until serving time.

Snowstorm Spaghetti and Meat Sauce

(6-8 servings)

"Henry, pick up some canned meat and bacon while you are on that side, and some spaghetti and tomato sauce. I'll get more chocolate and hot dogs and hamburgers and dry milk."
—Snowbound Mystery

What to Use

3 quarts water
1 Tablespoon cooking oil
12 ounces spaghetti (uncooked)
1 pound ground beef
1 can (32 ounce) spaghetti sauce
Parmesan cheese, grated

medium saucepan with lid
large saucepan with lid
pancake turner
measuring spoons
colander
tongs or pasta server
ladle or cup

What to Do

1. In large saucepan, bring water to a boil over high heat.
2. Cook meat in the medium saucepan over medium heat. Use a pancake turner to break meat apart as it cooks. When meat loses its red color, drain off the fat.
3. Add spaghetti sauce to the meat. Stir. Bring to a boil, stirring often. Cover and turn burner to low. Let the sauce simmer while you cook the spaghetti.
4. Carefully add the spaghetti to the boiling water. Add vegetable oil. Stir. Bring to a boil again.
5. Stir the spaghetti. Cover and turn off the burner. Let the spaghetti sit in the water for 15 minutes. The spaghetti will cook all by itself.
6. Drain the spaghetti in the colander. Carefully put the spaghetti back into the pan and cover until serving time.
7. To serve, take out a serving of spaghetti and put it on a plate. Ladle on sauce and sprinkle with Parmesan cheese.

Big Jeko's Pilaf

(4 servings)

The lunch was made of rice and lamb and onions and tomatoes and all sorts of delicious things, just what the Alden children liked.

—Bicycle Mystery

What to Use

1 cup rice, uncooked
2 cups water
1/2 pound ground lamb or beef
1 small onion, chopped
1/2 teaspoon cinnamon
1 dash nutmeg
1 can (16 ounces) tomatoes
2 teaspoons lemon juice
1/2 teaspoon salt

medium saucepan with lid
large saucepan with lid
knife
cutting board
pancake turner
measuring cups
measuring spoons
can opener
2-quart covered casserole
no-stick cooking spray

What to Do

1. Put rice and water in the medium saucepan. Cover. Bring to a boil over high heat. Turn heat to low and simmer 15-20 minutes.
2. In the large saucepan over medium heat, cook onions and meat until the meat loses its red color. Use a pancake turner to break the meat apart as it cooks. Drain off fat.
3. Preheat the oven to 350 degrees.
4. Add cooked rice, cinnamon, nutmeg, tomatoes, lemon juice, and salt to the meat mixture. Mix well.
5. Spray the casserole dish with no-stick cooking spray. Pour meat and rice mixture into the casserole dish. Cover and bake 25 minutes.

Larry's Secret Bean Recipe

(6 servings)

In *The Lighthouse Mystery*, Larry cooked a village supper that everyone in town enjoyed. He wouldn't tell anyone how he cooked his delicious baked beans and chowder.

What to Use

1 jar (48 ounces) great northern beans
1/2 pound smoked sausage, sliced
1 small onion, chopped
1 Tablespoon prepared mustard
1/2 cup brown sugar
1/2 cup maple-flavored syrup
1/3 cup ketchup
1/4 teaspoon pepper

2-quart casserole dish or slow-cooker with lid
cutting board
knife
measuring cups
measuring spoons
stirring spoon
no-stick cooking spray

What to Do

1. Spray the casserole dish or slow-cooker with no-stick cooking spray.
2. Put beans, with the liquid from the jar, and all the other ingredients into the casserole dish or slow cooker. Stir to mix well.
3. For a casserole dish, cover and bake in a 350-degree oven 2 1/2 hours. Uncover and bake another 1/2 hour.
4. For a slow-cooker, cover and cook on low 8 to 10 hours. During the last 1/2 hour, uncover and cook on high.

Beef Stew with Little Vegetables

(6-8 servings)

The girls were delighted with the meat and the little vegetables. With Henry's knife they cut the meat into little pieces.

—The Boxcar Children

What to Use

1 Tablespoon vegetable oil
1 pound beef stew meat
4 cups water
1 1/2 teaspoons salt
8 small carrots, scrubbed
8 small onions
1 cup celery, chopped
8-10 small potatoes, scrubbed
1 turnip, sliced (if wanted)
2 cups tomato juice
1/3 cup flour
1 cup more water

Dutch oven or soup kettle with lid
large stirring spoon
measuring cups
measuring spoons
cutting board
knife
vegetable brush
vegetable peeler
can opener

What to Do

1. Put oil and meat in the large pan and cook over medium heat until the meat is brown. Be sure to ask a grown-up to help with this.
2. Carefully add water and salt. Turn the heat to high and bring to a boil. Cover. Turn the heat to low and cook for 1 hour, or until meat is tender. Stir about every 15 minutes.
3. Prepare vegetables—scrub the carrots and potatoes, peel the onions, wash and chop the celery, and peel and slice the turnip (if wanted).
4. When the meat is tender, add the vegetables and tomato juice. Turn the heat to medium. Cook for about 20 minutes, or until the vegetables are tender.
5. Put 1 cup water and 1/3 cup flour into a pint jar. Cover tightly and shake until mixed. Add to stew. Stir. Cook, stirring often, until the stew thickens. This should take about 5 minutes.

Benny's Stuffed Fish

(6 servings)

Jessie piled the dressing made of bread, onions, melted butter, and salt on four pieces of fish. —Surprise Island

What to Use

1/2 cup margarine
1/4 cup chopped celery
1/4 cup chopped onion
1 2/3 cups water
1 package croutons
(6 ounces)
2 pounds plain, raw fish fillets*
2 Tablespoons lemon juice
1/4 teaspoon pepper

9" x 9" baking dish
no-stick cooking spray
cutting board
knife
measuring cup
measuring spoons
wooden spoon
paper towels
aluminum foil

What to Do

1. Melt 1/4 cup margarine over low heat. Add celery and onion and cook until soft. Carefully add water.
2. Add croutons and stir until croutons are moistened.
3. Preheat the oven to 350 degrees.
4. Rinse fish under cold running water. Pat dry with paper towels.
5. Spray baking dish with no-stick cooking spray. Put half the fish in the dish.
6. Spoon the stuffing over the fish. Place the remaining fish fillets over the stuffing.
7. Melt remaining 1/4 cup margarine. Stir in lemon juice and pepper. Spoon over the top layer of fish.
8. Cover with aluminum foil and bake 30 minutes or until the fish pulls apart easily in layers.

*You may use sole, turbot, or orange roughy.

Mike's Favorite Chicken Legs

(4 servings)

"Oh! Oh! Chicken legs!" yelled Benny, "I can eat a lot of those."
"How many can you eat?" asked Mrs. Cook.
"Well, four anyway," said Benny. "My friend Mike can eat eight."
—The Lighthouse Mystery

What to Use

8 chicken legs*
1 cup barbecue sauce

9" x 13" baking dish
no-stick cooking spray
measuring cup
pastry brush
tongs

What to Do

1. Preheat the oven to 350 degrees. Spray the baking dish with no-stick cooking spray.
2. Put chicken legs in a single layer in the baking dish.
3. Bake uncovered for 30 minutes.
4. Carefully remove the baking dish from the oven. Use the tongs to turn the chicken legs and brush all sides of each one with barbecue sauce. Pour the remaining sauce evenly over all the legs.
5. Bake uncovered for 15 minutes longer or until the chicken legs are tender and no longer pink inside.

*Or you can use other chicken pieces.

Golden Horn Pizza

(6-8 servings)

"I'm going to have a pizza," said Jessie.

"So am I," agreed Violet. "We haven't had a pizza for weeks and weeks." —Caboose Mystery

What to Use

1 Tablespoon cornmeal
1 Tablespoon flour
2 loaves frozen bread dough, thawed
vegetable oil or shortening
1 jar (15-16 ounces) pizza or spaghetti sauce
12 ounces shredded mozzarella cheese
1/2 cup grated Parmesan cheese

round pizza pan (15" across)
no-stick cooking spray
rolling pin
fork
spoon
measuring cups
measuring spoons
cutting board
knife
pizza cutter

Toppings for your pizza

3/4 pound cooked Italian sausage or ground beef, drained
1 cup sliced pepperoni
1 cup chopped ham
1 cup sliced mushrooms
1/2 cup chopped green pepper
1/4 cup chopped onion
1/4 cup sliced black olives

What to Do

1. Spray the pizza pan with no-stick cooking spray. Sprinkle cornmeal evenly over the pan.
2. Spread flour on the countertop and put the thawed dough on top of it. Squeeze the loaves together and form them into a big ball.
3. Put the dough in the pizza pan. Rub oil or shortening on your hands. Use your hands to spread the dough in the pan, being sure to go all the way to the edges.
4. Preheat the oven to 425 degrees.
5. Let the dough rest at least 10 minutes while you get the ingredients ready for the topping.
6. Poke the crust with a fork once in the middle and four more places around the edge. This will keep the dough from bubbling up. Bake for 7 minutes. Then remove from the oven.
7. Onto the partly baked crust, pour enough sauce to almost cover the crust. Spread the sauce with a spoon.
8. Add one or more of the toppings.
9. Sprinkle Parmesan and mozzarella cheeses on your pizza.
10. Put the pizza into the oven and bake 15 minutes.
11. Remove pizza from the oven. Cut with a pizza cutter and serve immediately.

New England Boiled Dinner

(6-8 servings)

Mrs. Randall went upstairs to make the beds. She had left all the things to make a boiled dinner. Corned beef, cabbage, carrots, and turnips lay on the table. —Bicycle Mystery

What to Use

4 pounds corned beef*
2 bay leaves
1 clove garlic, crushed
water
6 carrots, peeled
2 small turnips, peeled
6 red potatoes
6 onions, peeled
1 small cabbage, quartered

large kettle with lid
knife
vegetable peeler
large plate

What to Do

1. Put corned beef, bay leaves, and garlic into the kettle. Add enough water to cover the corned beef. Cover the kettle.
2. Bring to a boil over high heat. Turn the heat to low and simmer for about 3 1/2 hours until the meat is tender, adding more water when needed.
3. Scrub and prepare the vegetables. Cut and core the cabbage.
4. Add carrots, turnips, onions, and potatoes to meat. Boil for 20 minutes.
5. Add cabbage and cook everything 15 minutes more, or until the vegetables are tender. Remove the bay leaves. Serve the meat on a large plate with the vegetables all around it.

*Or you can use a 4-pound ham.

Lovan's Pot Roast

(6-8 servings)

It was a delicious pot roast cooking with turnips and carrots and onions and potatoes. —Mountain Top Mystery

What to Use

1/4 cup flour
1 teaspoon salt
1/2 teaspoon pepper
4-pound chuck roast
2 Tablespoons vegetable oil
1 cup water
2 turnips, peeled and quartered
8 small potatoes, cut in halves
8 carrots, cut in halves
8 small onions

large roasting pan with lid
measuring cups
measuring spoons
cutting board
small knife
vegetable peeler

What to Do

1. Preheat the oven to 325 degrees.
2. Mix flour, salt, and pepper together.
3. Rub the flour mixture on all sides of the roast.
4. Heat oil in the pan. Brown meat on both sides. Be sure to ask a grown-up to help with this.
5. Add water. Cover and roast in the oven 2-3 hours, or until the meat is tender. Add more water if necessary.
6. Scrub and prepare vegetables.
7. Carefully remove the pan from the oven. Put the vegetables in the pan with the meat. Cover the pan and return it to the oven.
8. Roast 1 hour longer, or until the vegetables are tender.

Hot Dog Animals

(4 servings)

On each plate was an animal made of a big frankfurter. The legs were four smaller sausages. The heads were pickles. The tails were carrot curls. —Caboose Mystery

What to Use

8 Vienna sausages
4 club frankfurters
1/2 cup water
2 small pickles
1 carrot

large saucepan with lid
small knife
vegetable peeler
tongs
plates

What to Do

1. Put sausages, frankfurters, and water in the saucepan.
2. Cover. Bring to a boil over high heat. Turn the burner down to low and simmer for 5 minutes.
3. Slice pickles in half lengthwise and use them to make the horses' heads. (You will have 4 halves.)
4. Peel the carrot with a vegetable peeler and cut in very thin strips. (These will be the horses' tails.)
5. Use tongs to remove the hot dogs and sausages from the pan. Cut the Vienna sausages in half lengthwise to make 16 legs.
6. Assemble the horses like this on the plates:

Campfire Cooking

The Alden Children love to camp out. They had their first camping adventure in *The Boxcar Children*. In the rest of the series, they cook many of their best meals over a campfire. There's nothing like fresh air to give you an appetite, and nothing like an open fire to give foods a wonderful flavor. Before trying any outdoor cooking, be sure to read the directions and safety rules on pages 56 and 57.

Campfire Safety Rules

Henry, Jessie, Violet, and Benny know that they have to follow safety rules when they cook over a campfire. Here are some safety rules for you to follow when you cook outside.

1. Always have an adult build your fire and stay with you when you are cooking over a campfire or on a grill.
2. Don't play with fire. Fires are very dangerous. Many people are hurt and much property is damaged each year because of carelessness with fires.
3. Always build small fires because they are easier to control.
4. Have a pail of water nearby to put out fires. If you don't have water, keep a pail of sand handy.
5. Don't run or play near a fire.
6. Don't wear loose clothing when cooking over an open fire.
7. If your clothes ever catch on fire, remember — STOP, DROP, and ROLL!
8. Don't throw aerosol cans or batteries into a fire. They can explode and cause severe injuries.
9. Before you leave your campsite, be sure that your fire is completely out. Douse the coals with water and bury them well under the soil so that no one will step on them by accident.

Lighten Up!

The Boxcar Children didn't have much cooking equipment when they lived in the boxcar, but they still cooked good food. If you take more equipment than you need when you camp out, you won't use it, and it will only get in your way. If you are planning to do any campfire cooking, an adult will, of course, need to take along matches and newspaper for fire building. You then should be able to get along with the items in this list:

frying pan with lid
plastic mixing bowl
mixing spoon
long-handled pancake turner
water pail
knife
fork
can opener
aluminum foil
vegetable brush
large pan for heating dishwater
paper towels
paper plates and cups
forks, knives, and spoons

Building a Campfire

Always have an adult build your fire for outdoor cooking. One kind of fire you can use is a hunter's fire. It is easy to make and gives steady heat. Ask the adult to follow these steps to make a hunter's fire:

1. On the ground, lay 2 green logs in a "V" shape about 10 inches apart at one end and 4 inches apart at the other end. The wider part of the V should face the wind.
2. Lay crumpled newspaper in the center of the V.
3. Top the paper with small, dry sticks.
4. Put larger sticks on top of the small ones.
5. Light the newspaper.
6. After the fire has started to burn, add larger pieces of wood to it.
7. To use the fire for cooking, let it burn down. Then cook over the red, glowing coals.

Using a Grill

Don't try to make a fire in an outdoor grill by yourself. Many outdoor grills come with their own directions. Have an adult follow these directions to make your fire in the grill.

Mountain Top Hamburgers

(6 servings)

Everybody had a job. The two boys built a fire, for even Benny knew how to start a good fire. The girls made cakes of the hamburger and took out the bacon. —Mountain Top Mystery

What to Use

6 slices cooked bacon or
 1 jar real bacon bits
1 1/2 pounds ground beef
6 cheese slices
hamburger buns

grill
long-handled pancake turner

What to Do

1. Read the safety rules and how-to steps for cooking with fire on pages 56 and 57. Have an adult start a fire in the grill.
2. Divide ground beef into 6 equal balls and form them into 1/2-inch thick patties.
3. When the coals have turned red, cook the hamburgers directly on the grill. Cook 8-10 minutes on each side.
4. Put the hamburger patties on the bun bottoms. Add cheese slices and then bacon. Put the top halves of the buns on the hamburgers.
5. Serve with any of the condiments and other ingredients for hamburgers that are listed for Jim's Place Hamburgers on page 37.

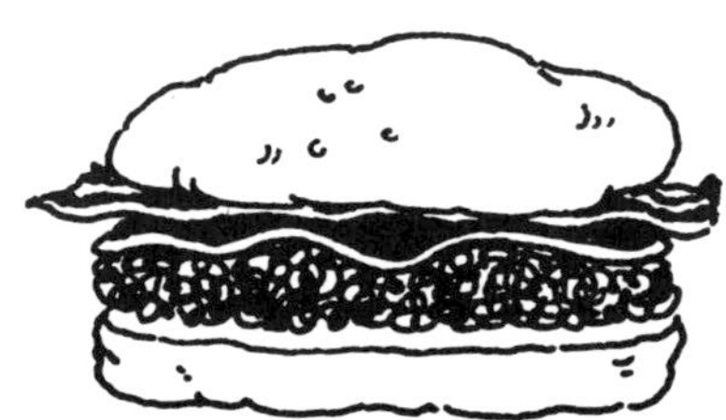

Cabin Hot Dogs on Sticks

(one for each person)

When the Aldens were safely in the cabin, Henry put more wood on the fire. Soon the place was warm and cozy. They sat around the fire cooking hot dogs on sticks. —Snowbound Mystery

What to Use

hot dogs
buns

1 long, green stick per person*

What to Do

1. Have an adult start a campfire or fire in the fireplace according to the directions and safety rules on pages 56 and 57. Allow the fire to die down and red coals to form.
2. Peel the bark from long, green sticks.
3. Pierce the hot dogs with sticks and cook slowly near the coals.
4. Put the hot dogs on the buns and add any of the condiments and other ingredients for hot dogs that are listed for Maggie's Hot Dogs on page 38.

Pigs in Blankets

To make pigs in blankets, use refrigerated biscuit dough for the blankets. Break off one biscuit for each hot dog. Roll dough between your hands into 12-inch long strings. Wrap dough strings around hot dogs and roast near the coals.

*You can also use a long hot-dog fork.

S'Mores

(1 serving)

After the Alden children ate hot dogs cooked over the fire in *Snowbound Mystery*, they may have eaten S'Mores. S'Mores got their name because they are so good that you always want to eat "some more." This recipe has peanut butter in it—especially for Benny.

What to Use

2 chocolate-covered graham crackers
1 marshmallow
1 teaspoon peanut butter

1 long, green stick
table knife

What to Do

1. Have an adult start a campfire or a fire in the grill. Be sure to read the directions and safety rules on pages 56 and 57 before cooking over hot coals.
2. Toast 1 marshmallow over hot coals.
3. Spread one side of a chocolate-covered graham cracker with peanut butter.
4. Put the roasted marshmallow on top of the peanut butter.
5. Put the other graham cracker on top of the marshmallow and squeeze just enough to hold everything together.

If you don't have chocolate-covered graham crackers, you can use plain graham crackers. Put an unwrapped chocolate kiss or piece of chocolate candy bar on top of the hot marshmallow before you add the top graham cracker.

Hobo Stew

(4 servings)

In *Caboose Mystery*, it was raining when Jessie and Violet wanted to make stew. They could have made hobo stew outside over a campfire in good weather.

What to Use

4 potatoes, scrubbed and sliced
1 medium onion, chopped
4 carrots, scrubbed and sliced
1 pound ground beef
1 Tablespoon margarine
salt and pepper

vegetable brush
cutting board
knife
aluminum foil

What to Do

1. Have an adult start a campfire or a fire in the grill. Be sure to read pages 56 and 57 before you start to cook on a grill or campfire.
2. For each serving, cut 2 large sheets of aluminum foil (about 17 inches long). Lay one sheet on top of the other. Spread a little margarine over the top sheet of foil.
3. Divide ground beef into four servings. Flatten beef to 1/2 inch thick on buttered side of foil.
4. Put 1 sliced potato, some chopped onion, and a sliced carrot on top of each portion of meat.
5. Put a small amount of margarine and a sprinkle of salt and pepper on each serving.
6. Wrap up each food bundle in double foil by bringing the 2 opposite ends up and folding them over several times. Fold the open ends over several times to keep juices from leaking out.
7. Put the bundles, folded side up, on the coals, on the grill, or in an oven set at 350 degrees. Cook for 1 hour.

Potato Camp Potatoes

(1 potato per serving)

On their canoe camping trip in *The Yellow House Mystery*, all the children had to eat were potatoes baked in a campfire. Afterward, they always called that place "Potato Camp."

What to Use

1 potato for each person
margarine
salt and pepper

large stick
vegetable brush
knife
aluminum foil
fork
spoon

What to Do

1. Have an adult build a campfire. Read the safety rules and directions on pages 56 and 57 before cooking on a campfire.
2. After the fire has died down and coals have turned red, use a stick to move the coals over to one side.
3. Scrub potatoes. Pierce each one four times with a fork to let steam escape. Wrap each potato in aluminum foil.
4. Put the potatoes where coals had been and use the stick to move coals over the top of the potatoes.
5. Bake the potatoes 1/2 to 1 hour. When the potatoes are done, they can be pierced easily with a knife.
6. Use a stick to roll the potatoes out of the fire. Then scoop out the insides with a spoon, or just eat the skin and all. Be careful! The potatoes are hot!
7. Serve with margarine and salt and pepper.

Salads and Vegetables

The Boxcar Children love salads and vegetables. They know that salads are nutritious and delicious, and they think that many salads are pretty enough to decorate the dinner table. Henry, Jessie, Violet, and Benny first had small vegetables from Dr. Moore's garden in *The Boxcar Children*. They ate peas from the garden on *Surprise Island*. Jessie and Violet helped Maggie cook asparagus for Aunt Jane in *The Woodshed Mystery*, and Al gave the children fresh sweet corn in *Caboose Mystery*. You'll enjoy adding some of the Boxcar Children's salads and vegetables to your lunches and dinners—maybe you'll even want to try peas for breakfast!

Tossed Salad

(8-10 servings)

A tossed salad could have been the centerpiece on the picnic table in *Benny Uncovers a Mystery.* Many colorful ingredients can be added to this salad to make it beautiful as well as tasty. Choose from two zesty salad dressings for the final delicious touch.

What to Use

1 head of lettuce
3 or more salad ingredients

cutting board
sharp knife
vegetable peeler
vegetable brush
large salad bowl
plastic wrap
salad forks or tongs

Salad Ingredients

tomato chunks
sliced radishes
sliced celery
sliced carrots
sliced mushrooms
sliced onion
sunflower seeds
bacon bits
grated cheese

What to Do

1. Use a knife to remove the core from the head of lettuce. Remove any damaged outside leaves.
2. Hold the lettuce under cold running water, cut side up, so that water goes into the lettuce. Drain, cut side down.
3. Tear lettuce leaves into bite-size pieces and put them in the salad bowl.
4. Prepare other ingredients by scrubbing, peeling, slicing, or doing whatever else needs to be done. Add the ingredients to the salad. Mix.
5. If you're not going to serve your salad right away, cover it with plastic wrap, and store it in the refrigerator.

Salad Dressings

What to Use for Red French Dressing

1/2 cup ketchup
1/2 cup vegetable oil
2 Tablespoons vinegar
2 Tablespoons sugar
1 Tablespoon chopped onion
2 Tablespoons lemon juice
1 teaspoon paprika

blender or pint jar with lid
measuring cup
measuring spoons
cutting board
knife
fruit juicer

What to Use for Italian Dressing

1 cup vegetable oil
1/4 cup vinegar
1/4 teaspoon garlic powder
1/2 teaspoon sugar
2 Tablespoons chopped onion
1 teaspoon dry mustard
1 teaspoon dry basil leaves
1/2 teaspoon dry oregano leaves

blender or pint jar with lid
measuring cup
measuring spoons
cutting board
knife

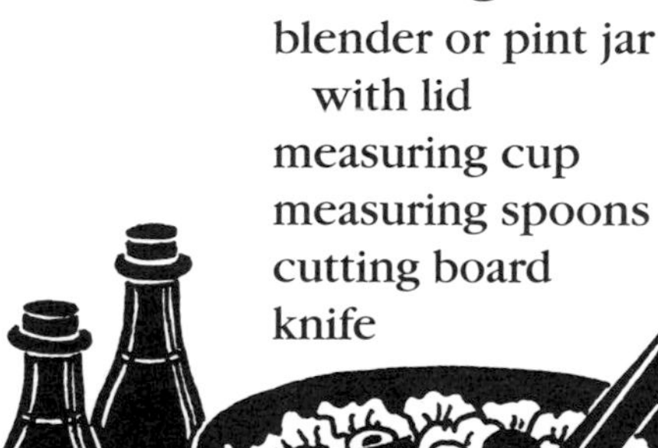

What to Do to Make Salad Dressings

1. Put all ingredients for the dressing you want to make into the blender container. Cover. Blend on high until smooth. Or you may put the ingredients in a covered pint jar and shake well. Be sure the lid is tightly fastened.
2. Refrigerate until ready to serve.

Violet's Apple-Nut Salad

(3-4 servings)

Jessie broke the nuts with her fingers. Violet chopped the apples with a knife. They mixed the two with salad dressing.
—Snowbound Mystery

What to Use

2 cups red apples, cubed
(3 or 4 apples)
1/4 cup walnuts, chopped
3 Tablespoons mayonnaise

mixing bowl
cutting board
small knife
measuring spoons
measuring cup
mixing spoon

What to Do

1. Wash the apples in cold water, cut in quarters, and cut out the cores. Do not peel. Cut the apples into 1/2-inch cubes.
2. Put apples, nuts, and mayonnaise in the mixing bowl. Mix.
3. Cover and chill before serving.

This type of salad is sometimes called Waldorf Salad. You may want to add one or more of the following ingredients. With each additional ingredient, add 1 Tablespoon mayonnaise to keep the salad moist.

1/2 cup dates, chopped
1/2 cup seedless raisins
1 cup celery, chopped
1 cup seedless grapes

Jessie's Potato Salad

(6 servings)

Jessie boiled a dozen eggs and a dozen potatoes. She put them in the refrigerator. By noon she had made an enormous potato salad.
—The Lighthouse Mystery

What to Use

4 medium potatoes
3 hard-boiled eggs*
1 cup celery, chopped
1/4 small onion, chopped
1/2 teaspoon salt
1/2 cup mayonnaise
1 teaspoon prepared mustard
paprika

vegetable brush
medium saucepan with lid
cutting board
knife
tongs
mixing bowl
measuring cup
measuring spoons
rubber scraper
stirring spoon

What to Do

1. Scrub potatoes under running water.
2. Put the potatoes in the saucepan. Add 2 cups water. Cover and bring to a boil over high heat. Turn the heat to low and simmer for 25-30 minutes.
3. Remove the potatoes with tongs and let them cool. Pull off the potato skins. Cut the potatoes into 1/2-inch cubes and put the cubes into the mixing bowl.
4. Add peeled, chopped hard-boiled eggs, celery, onion, salt, mayonnaise, and mustard. Mix well, scraping sides of bowl with the rubber scraper as you stir.
5. Sprinkle paprika on your potato salad for decoration.
6. Cover and refrigerate until serving time.

*You can find a recipe for hard-boiled eggs on page 30.

Benny's Mashed Potatoes

(4 servings)

"Oh, mashed potatoes!" shouted Benny. "You're a nice sister, Jessie! But where did you get them?"

"Out of a box," said Jessie. "It's instant potato."

—Houseboat Mystery

You can make instant mashed potatoes by following the directions on the box. Or you can use the following recipe to make your very own fresh mashed potatoes.

What to Use

6 to 8 potatoes
water
1/4 cup milk
1/4 cup margarine
salt (if wanted)

large saucepan with lid
vegetable peeler
cutting board
knife
measuring cup
colander
mixing bowl
potato masher or electric mixer

What to Do

1. Peel potatoes and wash them in cold water. Cut each potato into quarters.
2. Put the potatoes into the saucepan and cover them with cold water.
3. Bring to a boil over high heat. Turn the heat down to medium and cook covered for 20 minutes, or until potatoes are soft.
4. Drain in the colander. Put the potatoes into a mixing bowl. Add milk, margarine, and salt (if wanted).
5. Mash with a potato masher. If you want fluffy mashed potatoes, break them up with a fork and then beat them with an electric mixer until they are light and fluffy.

Al's Corn on the Cob

(4 servings)

The engineer in *Caboose Mystery* had a whole field of sweet corn. He told Al to let the children pick all they wanted. Al told Violet that corn is best when it's cooked as soon as it's picked. He was right!

What to Use

4 ears fresh sweet corn
2 cups water
margarine
salt (if wanted)

large kettle with lid
measuring cup
tongs
large serving plate

What to Do

1. Husk corn and remove silk.
2. Put water in the kettle. You should have about 1 inch of water in the kettle. Add more water if you need to.
3. Put corn in the kettle. Cover. Bring to a boil over high heat. Turn the heat down to medium and steam the corn for 15 minutes. Steaming helps keep the corn crisp, sweet, and nutritious.
4. Remove with tongs and place on a large serving plate.
5. Serve with margarine and salt (if wanted).

How to Microwave

1. Put 4 ears of corn in a single layer in a glass baking dish. Add 1/4 cup water.
2. Cover with plastic wrap. Poke 3 or 4 holes in the wrap with a fork to let the steam out.
3. Cook on high 12 to 15 minutes, turning dish 1/4 turn after 6 minutes.

Aunt Jane's Favorite Asparagus

(4 servings)

In *The Woodshed Mystery*, Maggie cooked one of Aunt Jane's favorite vegetables, early asparagus.

What to Use

1 pound fresh asparagus
1/2 cup water
1 Tablespoon margarine, melted
1 teaspoon lemon juice

medium saucepan with lid
colander
cutting board
knife
measuring cup
measuring spoons

What to Do

1. Wash asparagus in cold water. Drain in colander.
2. Trim 1 1/2 inches from the cut ends of the asparagus stalks so that no tough parts are left.
3. Cut asparagus into two-inch pieces.
4. Put asparagus and water into saucepan. Cover. Bring to a boil over high heat.
5. Turn the heat to low and simmer for 15 minutes. Drain. Mix margarine and lemon juice. Pour over asparagus in a serving dish.

For microwave directions, see page 72.

Surprise Island Peas

(4 servings)

"Oh, look," cried Benny. "Peas! I'd like peas for dinner!"
—Surprise Island

What to Use

2 cups frozen peas*
1/2 cup water
1 Tablespoon margarine

medium saucepan with lid
measuring cup
measuring spoons
colander

What to Do

1. Bring water to a boil over high heat.
2. Add peas and continue cooking on high until the water boils again.
3. Cook the peas for 2 or 3 minutes in boiling water. Do not boil them longer or they will lose their bright green color and become mushy.
4. Drain in the colander and serve with margarine.

*You can use fresh peas for this recipe. If you do, you will have to shell the peas before you cook them. Bring the peas to a boil. Then turn the heat down and simmer for 10 minutes.

For microwave directions, see page 72.

Henry's Boxcar Carrots

(4 servings)

When Henry worked in Mrs. Moore's garden in *The Boxcar Children*, Mrs. Moore gave him little carrots and other small vegetables to take home.

What to Use

1/2 pound carrots
(4 or 5 carrots)
1/2 cup water
1 Tablespoon margarine

medium saucepan with lid
vegetable peeler
measuring spoons
measuring cup
colander

What to Do

1. Wash, peel, and slice carrots.
2. Put carrots and water into the saucepan. Cover. Bring to a boil over high heat. Turn the heat down to low and simmer for 20 minutes.
3. Drain in the colander and serve with margarine.

How to Microwave Vegetables

Put prepared vegetables, water, and seasonings into a glass or plastic dish. Cover with plastic wrap and cook on high for the following times:

asparagus — 9 to 11 minutes
peas — 6 to 8 minutes
carrots — 7 to 10 minutes

Cookies and Cakes

The Boxcar Children love cookies. Henry brought cookies to the boxcar from Dr. Moore's house in *The Boxcar Children*. And in *The Woodshed Mystery*, they ate round white cookies with holes in the middle. When the Aldens have something to celebrate, they often serve a cake. Benny's and Aunt Jane's birthdays are very special celebrations indeed. For a party or to make an ordinary day more fun, surprise your family and friends with a delicious cake you've made yourself.

Benny's Peanut Butter Peaks

(3 dozen)

Benny loves peanut butter so much that he just has to love these cookies, too.

What to Use

1 stick softened margarine (1/2 cup)
1/2 cup peanut butter
1/2 cup sugar
1/2 cup brown sugar
1 egg
1 1/4 cups flour
3/4 teaspoon baking soda
1/2 teaspoon baking powder
3 Tablespoons more sugar
36 chocolate kisses, unwrapped

large mixing bowl
measuring cups
measuring spoons
electric mixer
rubber scraper
mixing spoon
plastic wrap
cookie sheet
no-stick cooking spray
small plastic bag
pancake turner
cooling rack

What to Do

1. Put margarine, peanut butter, 1/2 cup sugar, brown sugar, and egg into the large mixing bowl. Beat with electric mixer on medium until smooth and creamy.
2. Mix in flour, baking soda, and baking powder. Cover and chill for 1 hour or more.
3. Preheat the oven to 375 degrees. Spray cookie sheet with no-stick cooking spray.
4. Put the 3 Tablespoons of sugar in a plastic bag.
5. Shape the dough into balls about the size of walnuts in the shell. Shake three balls at a time in the plastic bag. Place cookies 2 inches apart on the cookie sheet.
6. Bake 8 minutes. Put a chocolate kiss in the center of each cookie and press down gently. Continue baking 2-4 minutes, or until chocolate has melted down a little.
7. Remove cookies with pancake turner and cool on cooling rack.

Round White Cookies with Holes in the Middle

(4 dozen cookies)

They were big round white cookies with holes in the middle. They were brown around the edges. How good they smelled!
—The Woodshed Mystery

What to Use

1 1/2 sticks softened margarine (3/4 cup)
1 cup sugar
2 eggs
1 teaspoon vanilla
2 1/2 cups flour
1 teaspoon baking powder
1/2 teaspoon salt

measuring cups
measuring spoons
large mixing bowl
electric mixer
mixing spoon
rolling pin
doughnut cutter
cookie sheet
pancake turner
cooling rack
sifter

What to Do

1. Put margarine, sugar, eggs, and vanilla in the mixing bowl. Beat with an electric mixer on medium until smooth.
2. Add flour, baking powder, and salt. Mix well.
3. Cover and refrigerate for 1 hour or overnight.
4. Preheat the oven to 400 degrees.
5. Use a rolling pin to roll the dough to 1/4 inch thick.
6. Cut out cookies with a doughnut cutter dipped in flour.
7. Put cookies 2 inches apart on an ungreased cookie sheet.
8. Bake for 8 minutes.
9. Remove the cookies with a pancake turner and cool on a cooling rack. Frost with White Frosting on page 77.

White Frosting

This frosting will make your big round cookies with holes in the middle into big round *white* cookies with holes in the middle.

What to Use

2 Tablespoons softened margarine
1 1/2 cups powdered sugar
1/2 teaspoon vanilla
1 Tablespoon milk

measuring cup
measuring spoons
small mixing bowl
mixing spoon
electric mixer
table knife

What to Do

1. Put margarine and powdered sugar in the mixing bowl. Mix well.
2. Add vanilla and milk. Beat on medium until smooth.
3. Use a knife to put a thin layer of frosting on the cooled cookies.

Dr. Moore's Favorite Brown Cookies

(5 dozen cookies)

Henry laughed at Benny and pulled the bag out of his pocket. In it were ten delicious brown cookies. —The Boxcar Children

What to Use

- 1 1/3 cups softened margarine
- 2 cups brown sugar
- 2 eggs
- 3 cups flour
- 1 teaspoon baking soda
- 2 teaspoons vanilla
- 1 large bag (12 ounces) chocolate chips
- 1 cup chopped nuts (if wanted)

- mixing bowl
- measuring cups
- measuring spoons
- electric mixer
- mixing spoon
- rubber scraper
- teaspoon
- cookie sheet
- pancake turner
- cooling rack

What to Do

1. Preheat the oven to 375 degrees.
2. Put margarine, sugar, and eggs in the mixing bowl. Beat with electric mixer on medium until smooth.
3. Add flour, baking soda, and vanilla. Mix well.
4. Stir in chocolate chips and nuts (if wanted). Dough will be very stiff.
5. Put teaspoonfuls of dough 2 inches apart on an ungreased cookie sheet. Use the rubber scraper to get all the dough out of the bowl.
6. Bake 8-10 minutes for soft cookies; 10 to 12 minutes for crisp cookies.
7. Use a pancake turner to take cookies off the cookie sheet. Cool on cooling rack.

Lighthouse Brownies

(16 brownies)

In *The Lighthouse Mystery*, Benny ate brownies while trying to figure out a clue. You can make these brownies in a microwave or conventional oven.

What to Use

1 stick margarine, melted
1/2 cup unsweetened cocoa
1 cup sugar
2 eggs
3/4 cup flour
1 teaspoon vanilla
1/2 cup chopped nuts (if wanted)

mixing bowl
measuring cups
measuring spoons
stirring spoon
9" x 9" glass baking dish
small saucepan
no-stick cooking spray
toothpicks

What to Do

1. Put margarine in the mixing bowl and cook in the microwave oven on low 1 minute or until melted.
2. Add cocoa and sugar. Mix well.
3. Add eggs, flour, vanilla, and nuts (if wanted). Mix well and pour into the baking dish.
4. Cook in the microwave oven* on high 6-7 minutes, turning 1/4 turn every 2 minutes. When brownies are done, the top will look dry and spring back when touched.

*To bake in conventional oven, preheat oven to 350 degrees. Melt margarine in saucepan over low heat. Spray the baking dish with no-stick spray. Bake 25-30 minutes or until toothpick poked in center comes out clean.

Benny's Birthday Cake

(12-15 servings)

"Benny," said Jessie. "Violet is going to bake you a birthday cake before she takes her lesson."

"Is she?" asked Benny, giving a last yell. "I want to watch her make my cake."

Violet got out her cooking things. She laid everything she needed on the pie-board. —Surprise Island

What to Use

2 1/2 cups flour
1 3/4 cups sugar
1/2 cup unsweetened cocoa
2 teaspoons baking soda
1/2 cup vegetable oil
2 Tablespoons white vinegar
2 teaspoons vanilla
1 3/4 cups water
1 carton (8 ounces) whipped topping, thawed

2 round 9"cake pans
large mixing bowl
electric mixer
measuring cups
measuring spoons
rubber scraper
no-stick cooking spray
table knife
toothpicks
plastic wrap
2 large dinner plates
wire cooling rack

What to Do

1. Preheat the oven to 350 degrees. Spray the cake pans with no-stick cooking spray.
2. Put flour, sugar, cocoa, and baking soda into the mixing bowl. Mix on low until well blended.
3. Add cooking oil, vinegar, vanilla, and water. Mix on medium until smooth. Scrape sides and bottom of the bowl with the rubber scraper to make sure all ingredients are blended.

4. Divide the batter evenly between the cake pans.
5. Bake 35 to 40 minutes. Test by sticking a toothpick into the center of each layer. If the toothpicks come out clean, the cake is done.
6. Cool 15 minutes on a wire rack.

Remove cake layers from the pans

1. Use a table knife to cut around the edge of each cake pan to loosen the cake layer. Put a plate upside down on one layer and turn the cake layer and plate over. The layer will be upside down on the plate.
2. Put a piece of plastic wrap over the second cake layer. Put the second plate on top of the plastic wrap. Flip.
3. Let the cakes cool completely.

Frost the cake

1. Begin with the cake layer that does not have plastic wrap. Spread whipped topping on top of this layer.
2. Using the plastic wrap, pick up the second layer and turn it over on top of the first layer. Remove the plastic wrap.
3. Spread whipped topping on the top and sides of the cake. If you are not going to serve your cake within 5 hours, don't put the frosting on now. Put plastic wrap on the cake and store it in the refrigerator until serving time. Then frost the cake.

If you want your cake to look just like Benny's birthday cake, put candles and a small, clean, plastic toy dog on top. Happy Birthday, Benny!

Rocking Horse Cake

(15 servings)

In *Tree House Mystery*, Uncle Max made this special cake. Read the book to find out why he decorated his cake with a rocking horse.

What to Use

1/2 cup softened margarine (1 stick)
1 cup sugar
2 eggs
1/2 cup milk
1 teaspoon vanilla
1 3/4 cups flour
1 Tablespoon baking powder
1/4 teaspoon salt

9" x 13" cake pan
no-stick cooking spray
large mixing bowl
measuring cups
measuring spoons
electric mixer
rubber scraper
toothpicks
cooling rack

What to Do

1. Preheat the oven to 350 degrees. Spray the cake pan with no-stick cooking spray.
2. Put margarine, sugar, and eggs into the mixing bowl. Beat on medium until smooth.
3. Add milk and vanilla. Beat on low to mix. Add flour, baking powder, and salt. Beat on medium until light and smooth.
4. Pour batter into cake pan.
5. Bake 35 minutes. Test by sticking a toothpick into the center of the cake. If the toothpick comes out clean, the cake is done. Cool completely before frosting.
6. Use White Frosting on page 77 to frost this cake.

The Rocking Horse

You can make your cake look like the one Uncle Max made.

1. Trace this rocking horse on a sheet of paper.
2. Cut out the traced rocking horse and carefully lay it on top of the frosted cake.
3. Trace around the paper with a toothpick to make guidelines.
4. Remove the paper from the cake.
5. Use any color decorator frosting in a tube to outline the rocking horse. Then fill in the outline with more frosting.
6. Use green frosting in a tube to draw leaves on your cake and pink frosting in a tube to make roses.

Aunt Jane's Birthday Cake

(12 servings)

They set eight places with Aunt Jane's best dishes. The birthday cake had seventy candles on it. —Mystery Ranch

What to Use

2 cups shredded carrots
3 eggs
1 cup vegetable oil
2 cups flour
2 teaspoons cinnamon
1 1/2 cups sugar
2 teaspoons baking powder
1 teaspoon baking soda
1 teaspoon vanilla
1 cup crushed pineapple with juice

9" x 13" cake pan
no-stick cooking spray
vegetable shredder
large mixing bowl
wire whisk
measuring cups
measuring spoons
can opener
rubber scraper
toothpicks

What to Do

1. Preheat oven to 350 degrees. Spray cake pan with no-stick cooking spray.
2. Put all of the ingredients into the mixing bowl. Mix with a wire whisk until well blended.
3. Pour the batter into the cake pan. Bake 45 minutes.
4. Cool before frosting.

To frost your cake, make 2 batches of White Frosting on page 77, but use 1 package (3 ounces) cream cheese instead of the margarine — 1/2 package of cream cheese for each batch.

Desserts

The Aldens know that dessert doesn't always have to be cookies or cake. Sometimes they eat fresh fruit for dessert. Sometimes they have one of their other favorite scrumptious sweet treats. Try one of these Boxcar favorites—your whole family will cheer!

Miner's Blueberry Pie

(6-8 servings)

When the whistle blew at noon, the men came pouring out of the mine. They saw the new sign and they all wanted hot pies. Soon all the pies were sold. —Mike's Mystery

What to Use

2 frozen deep dish piecrusts, thawed
3 cups fresh or frozen blueberries
1/3 cup sugar
1/4 cup flour
1/2 teaspoon cinnamon
1 Tablespoon margarine

measuring cup
measuring spoons
large mixing bowl
mixing spoon
fork
knife

What to Do

1. Preheat the oven to 400 degrees.
2. Put blueberries, sugar, flour, and cinnamon into the mixing bowl. Stir gently.
3. Pour blueberry mixture into one of the piecrusts.
4. Cut margarine into small pieces. Put them on top of the blueberry mixture.
5. Wet your fingers with cold water and run them along the top edge of the bottom piecrust.
6. Turn the remaining crust upside down on top of the blueberries and remove the pan. Use a fork to press the edges of the two crusts together.
7. Cut slits in the top crust to let steam escape. Bake 40-50 minutes or until lightly browned.

Tree House Chocolate Pudding

(4 servings)

In *Tree House Mystery*, Mrs. Beach sent dinner up to Henry, Benny, and the new neighbor boys in the tree house. She even sent up a bowl of delicious chocolate pudding for dessert.

What to Use

3 Tablespoons unsweetened cocoa
1/2 cup sugar
3 Tablespoons cornstarch
2 cups milk

medium saucepan with lid
measuring cups
measuring spoons
wooden spoon

What to Do

1. Put cocoa, sugar, and cornstarch into the saucepan. Mix until well blended.
2. Add milk to cocoa mixture. Stir until dry ingredients are dissolved.
3. Cook over medium heat, stirring constantly until mixture starts to boil. Boil for 1 minute. Remove from heat.
4. Cover the pan and let cool, or serve warm. After the pudding has cooled to room temperature, it MUST be refrigerated.

Mrs. McGregor's Orange Pudding

(6 servings)

In *Tree House Mystery*, Mrs. McGregor gave Benny orange pudding to take to the new neighbors who had moved in next door.

What to Use

3 eggs
1/2 cup flour
1/2 teaspoon baking powder
1/4 teaspoon salt
2 Tablespoons margarine, melted
1/4 cup sweet orange marmalade
1 1/2 cups milk

2-quart baking dish
no-stick cooking spray
large mixing bowl
measuring cups
measuring spoons
wire whisk

What to Do

1. Preheat the oven to 350 degrees. Spray the baking dish with no-stick cooking spray.
2. Break eggs into the large mixing bowl and beat with the wire whisk until well blended.
3. Add flour, baking powder, and salt. Mix well with the whisk.
4. Add melted margarine and orange marmalade. Mix well.
5. Stir in milk.
6. Pour the mixture into the baking dish. Bake 45 minutes, or until knife poked in the center comes out clean. Chill before serving.

Jessie's Apple Pie

(6 servings)

Everyone loves apple pie! You can use this "easy as pie" recipe to make your own apple pie. Serve it warm with ice cream or the way Henry likes it, with a slice of cheese.

What to Use

2 frozen deep-dish piecrusts, thawed
5 cups apples, peeled, sliced, and cored
1/2 cup sugar
3 Tablespoons flour
1/2 teaspoon cinnamon
dash of nutmeg
dash of salt
1 Tablespoon margarine

large mixing bowl
vegetable peeler
small knife
cutting board
measuring cup
measuring spoons
mixing spoon
fork

What to Do

1. Preheat the oven to 400 degrees.
2. Prepare the apples by peeling, coring, and slicing them.
3. Put apple slices, sugar, flour, cinnamon, nutmeg, and salt in the mixing bowl. Stir to mix well. Put into one of the piecrusts.
4. Cut margarine into small pieces and put them on top of the apple slices.
5. Wet your fingers with cold water and run them along the top edge of the bottom piecrust.
6. Turn the remaining crust upside down on top of the apples and remove the top pan. Use a fork to press the edges of the two crusts together.
7. Cut slits in the top crust to let steam escape. Bake 40-50 minutes or until lightly browned.

Hollow-Leg Bread Pudding

(6-8 servings)

"I'm going to have bread pudding for dessert."

"I hope you can hold all that food," said Grandfather, looking at him.

"Oh, I can," said Benny. "I have a hollow leg."

—Mountain Top Mystery

What to Use

1/2 cup brown sugar
1/2 teaspoon cinnamon
1/4 teaspoon salt
2 teaspoons vanilla
2 eggs
1/2 cup raisins
2 cups milk
6 slices stale bread

9" pie pan
no-stick cooking spray
large mixing bowl
measuring cup
measuring spoons
mixing spoon
quart jar with lid

What to Do

1. Preheat oven to 350 degrees. Spray pie pan with no-stick cooking spray.
2. Mix brown sugar, cinnamon, and salt in the mixing bowl.
3. Add vanilla, eggs, raisins, and milk. Mix well.
4. Tear the bread into pieces and add it to the mixture. Stir gently until bread soaks up all the liquid.
5. Bake 45 minutes or until knife poked into the center comes out clean. Pudding will look all puffed up, but it will go down as it cools. Serve warm or cool.

You can use Jessie's Eggnog on page 16 as a sauce for your bread pudding. Do not sprinkle the nutmeg on the eggnog.

Snow Ice Cream

(10 servings)

In *Snowbound Mystery*, the Alden children were snowed in at the cabin. They had to make do with what they had. As a surprise for the boys, Violet thought of Snow Ice Cream. It is quick and easy to make.

What to Use

- 1/2 cup milk
- 14 ounce can sweetened condensed milk
- 3 large eggs
- 1/4 teaspoon salt
- 1 cup sugar
- 1 Tablespoon vanilla
- 2 gallons (or more) very fresh, light, fluffy snow

- saucepan with lid
- can opener
- measuring cups
- measuring spoons
- wire whisk
- large mixing bowl*
- electric mixer
- large container for snow

What to Do

1. Put milk, sweetened condensed milk, eggs, and salt in the saucepan. Mix with a wire whisk until smooth.
2. Cook over medium heat, stirring constantly with the whisk until the mixture just begins to boil.
3. Remove from heat and add sugar and vanilla.
4. Cover and let cool in the refrigerator.
5. When the mixture is about room temperature, pour it into a large mixing bowl. Add 1 quart of snow and mix. Continue adding more snow until the mixture is very thick and looks like ice cream. Be careful not to add too much snow. Serve right away.

*You may use a clean dishpan if you don't have a large bowl.
Use only very fresh, light, fluffy snow.

Mary's Cherry Dumplings

(4-6 servings)

In *The Boxcar Children*, Mary, Dr. Moore's cook, made cherry dumplings from the cherries in Dr. Moore's orchard.

What to Use

1 Tablespoon flour
1 tube (8 ounces) refrigerator crescent rolls
1 can (21 ounces) cherry pie filling
2 teaspoons sugar

9" x 13" baking dish
no-stick cooking spray
rolling pin
measuring cup
measuring spoons
pancake turner

What to Do

1. Preheat oven to 400 degrees. Spray baking dish with no-stick cooking spray. Set aside until needed.
2. Dust the countertop with flour. Open the crescent roll tube and unroll the dough onto the floured countertop. Divide the dough on dividing lines into 4 rectangles. Turn the squares over so that both sides are floured. Using a rolling pin, roll each piece of dough into a larger (6" x 6") square.
3. Put 1/3 cup of the pie filling in the center of each dough square. Wet your fingers with cold water and run your fingers around the edge of the dough square. This will help seal the dumplings.
4. To seal each dumpling, bring opposite corners up over the cherry filling and pinch together. Do the same with the other 2 corners. Pinch edges of dough together to seal. Put dumplings in the baking dish. Sprinkle 1/2 teaspoon sugar on each dumpling.
5. Bake 20-25 minutes, or until golden brown. Cool before serving.

Henry, Jessie, Violet, and Benny hope you enjoy using their favorite recipes. You can use the recipes often to prepare meals or favorite dishes for your family. And the whole family can have fun cooking together!

Don't forget your friends! Homemade cookies—Dr. Moore's Favorite Brown Cookies, Benny's Peanut Butter Peaks, Round White Cookies with Holes in the Middle, and Lighthouse Brownies—make delicious holiday gifts.

Index